CENGAGE Learning

Novels for Students, Volume 8

Staff

Series Editor: Deborah A. Stanley.

Contributing Editors: Peg Bessette, Sara L. Constantakis, Catherine L. Goldstein, Dwayne D. Hayes, Motoko Fujishiro Huthwaite, Arlene M. Johnson, Angela Yvonne Jones, James E. Person, Jr., Polly Rapp, Erin White.

Editorial Technical Specialist: Tim White.

Managing Editor: Joyce Nakamura.

Research: Victoria B. Cariappa, *Research Team Manager*. Andy Malonis, *Research Specialist*. Tamara C. Nott, Tracie A. Richardson, and Cheryl L. Warnock, *Research Associates*. Jeffrey Daniels, *Research Assistant*.

Permissions: Susan M. Trosky, *Permissions Manager*. Maria L. Franklin, *Permissions Specialist*. Sarah Tomacek, *Permissions Associate*.

Production: Mary Beth Trimper, *Production Director*. Evi Seoud, *Assistant Production Manager*. Cindy Range, *Production Assistant*.

Graphic Services: Randy Bassett, *Image Database Supervisor*. Robert Duncan and Michael Logusz, *Imaging Specialists*. Pamela A. Reed, *Photography Coordinator*. Gary Leach, *Macintosh Artist*.

Product Design: Cynthia Baldwin, *Product Design Manager*. Cover Design: Michelle DiMercurio, *Art Director*. Page Design: Pamela A. E. Galbreath, *Senior Art Director*.

Copyright Notice

Since this page cannot legibly accommodate all copyright notices, the acknowledgments constitute an extension of the copyright notice.

While every effort has been made to secure permission to reprint material and to ensure the reliability of the information presented in this publication, Gale Research neither guarantees the accuracy of the data contained herein nor assumes any responsibility for errors, omissions, or discrepancies. Gale accepts no payment for listing; and inclusion in the publication of any organization, agency, institution, publication, service, or individual does not imply endorsement of the editors or publisher. Errors brought to the attention of the publisher and verified to the satisfaction of the publisher will be corrected in future editions.

This publication is a creative work fully protected by all applicable copyright laws, as well as by misappropriation, trade secret, unfair competition, and other applicable laws. The authors and editors of this work have added value to the underlying factual material herein through one or more of the following: unique and original selection, coordination, expression, arrangement, and classification of the information. All rights to this publication will be vigorously defended.

Copyright © 2000
The Gale Group
27500 Drake Rd.
Farmington Hills, MI 48331-3535

All rights reserved including the right of reproduction in whole or in part in any form.

ISBN 0-7876-3827-7
ISSN 1094-3552

Printed in the United States of America.
10 9 8 7 6 5 4 3 2 1

Empire of the Sun

J. G. Ballard 1984

Introduction

When *Empire of the Sun* was published in 1984, it quickly became a critical and commercial success. Many commentators regard it as one of the finest war novels ever written. In the novel, Ballard chronicles the semi-autobiographical experiences of an eleven-year-old British boy named Jim living in China during World War II.

When the fighting comes to Shanghai, Jim is separated from his parents and sent to a prison camp. It is there that he faces the harsh realities of war and learns important lessons about human nature. The novel has been praised for its vivid portrayal of the devastating effects of war and the psychology of survival as seen through the eyes of a young boy. In this moving coming-of-age tale, Jim lets go of his innocent ideas about war and heroism and in the process reveals the meaning of courage, tenacity, and faith in the endurance of the human spirit.

Author Biography

J. G. Ballard was born on November 15, 1930, in Shanghai. Like Jim, the protagonist of *Empire of the Sun*, Ballard was a child when World War II began; and, like Jim, he wandered the city of Shanghai after being separated from his parents. However, he was eventually reunited with them in Lunghua prison camp, where the three remained prisoners until the camp was liberated by the American army.

Ballard left China when he was sixteen and later studied medicine at Cambridge University from 1949 to 1951. He became a regular contributor to *New Worlds* magazine. From 1954 to 1957 he served as a pilot for the Royal Air Force.

Ballard married Helen Matthews in 1953 and had three children. Her death in 1964 devastated him and death became a recurring theme in his writing. He began writing science fiction in the mid-1950s and, by the 1960s, he became associated with the "New Wave" movement in science fiction, which introduced experimental literary techniques and more sophisticated subject matter into the genre. Initially his novels did not garner much critical or commercial success. Eventually, he was recognized as an innovative writer of science fiction, especially in England and Europe.

Ballard departed from the science fiction genre in several of his short stories and in *Empire of the*

Sun and its sequel, *The Kindness of Women* (1991), which deals with Ballard's life in England after the war. *Empire of the Sun* was a popular and critical success, earning a Guardian Fiction Prize in 1984, a nomination for the Booker Prize in 1984, and the James Tait Black Memorial Prize in 1985. Adapted into a movie in 1987, the film was produced and directed by Steven Spielberg. Ballard's fifteen novels and numerous short stories have established him not only as a first-rate science fiction writer, but also as an accomplished novelist and short story writer of works that explore intricate psychological landscapes.

Plot Summary

Part I

The novel opens on the day Japan attacked Pearl Harbor, December 7, 1941, in Shanghai's International Settlement. Eleven-year-old Jamie—or Jim as he prefers to be called—his father and his mother live in a wealthy European area within the city.

With the threat of war, most of the European women and children have been evacuated to Hong Kong and Singapore. Jim's family remains. While riding his bicycle through the streets of Shanghai, he dreams of being a fighter pilot like the Japanese pilots that fly over the city.

On the morning of the 7th, Jim witnesses the Japanese attack on British and American warships docked at Shanghai (which occurred at the same time as the attack on Pearl Harbor), and in the ensuing turmoil he becomes separated from his parents.

After the attack, the Japanese intern the Europeans living in the city. For the next few months, Jim roams the city on his bicycle in constant search for food, shelter, and a recognizable face. Exhausted from long trips around the city and a lack of food, he decides to give himself up to the Japanese.

As he roams the city, Jim meets Frank and Basie, two American sailors. The three are soon captured and Basie and Jim are sent to a detention center. On arrival at the camp, Jim becomes seriously ill. With Basie's help, he learns how to get enough food to keep himself alive.

Part II

Jim and Basie are transported outside the city to the prison camp at Lunghua. During his three years there, Jim faces hunger, disease, and death. As the American bombing raids intensify, their meager rations are reduced.

Jim spends his time running errands for Basie, Dr. Ransome, and others. He tries to ingratiate himself with both prisoners and guards to gain company, food, and gifts, like a shiny pair of golf shoes. However, his boundless energy and unflagging determination to survive sometimes annoy the other prisoners.

He enjoys visiting the American prisoners, and reads copies of *Reader's Digest* and *Popular Mechanics*. He plays chess and does homework problems assigned by Dr. Ransome. Over time, he forgets what his parents looked like.

In August 1945, after American air attacks become a daily event, the Japanese evacuate the camp to the Olympic Stadium outside Shanghai. Jim finds it hard to leave the relative security of the camp. During the difficult journey there, many of the prisoners die. At one point, Jim becomes seduced by the idea of death, and decides to stop along the side of the road. Mr. Maxted, however, coaxes him on, insisting, "we need you to lead the way."

Mr. Maxted dies after they are herded inside the stadium. Jim acknowledges that "he had been trying to keep the war alive, and with it the security he had known in the camp. Now it was time to rid himself of Lunghua, and face up squarely to the present, however uncertain, the one rule that had sustained him through the years of the war."

Part III

That night the Japanese soldiers vanish and Jim sees a strange flash of light that floods the stadium. Later he is told the light came from the atomic bomb explosion at Nagasaki, reflected across the China Sea. Not knowing where to go, Jim decides to walk back to Lunghua.

As he walks back to Lunghua, American planes drop canisters of food and magazines that contain tales of the heroic exploits of the American soldiers. Jim devours the food and eagerly reads the magazines; the cans of Spam and candy bars make the "most satisfying" meal of his life. Back in the camp, unsure of what to do next, he notes that "peace had come, but it failed to fit properly." At times he is not sure that the war is really over.

Jim soon leaves with Lieutenant Price, an American who had taken control of Lunghua. Price, however makes a detour to the Olympic Stadium, hoping to steal some looted cars and furniture. After they arrive, a Chinese soldier shoots Price. As a threatening gang of bandits surrounds Jim, he recognizes Basie among them. After Basie and the gang strand him on a mud flat, he returns to the camp where he is reunited with Dr. Ransome.

Two months later Jim has been reunited with his parents and is preparing for his departure for England. As his parents slowly recover from their years at a prison camp in Soochow, Jim returns by bicycle to his old haunts in the city. He realizes that "only part of his mind would leave Shanghai. The rest would remain there forever, returning on the tide like the coffins launched from the funeral piers at Nantao."

Characters

Basie

Basie is an American sailor. Jim meets him before the two of them are sent to the prison camp and describes Basie as having a "bland, unmarked face from which all the copious experiences of his life had been cleverly erased." Basie is a player and tries to make money off of the war by trading anything he can. As a result, he acquires "a complete general store" at the camp.

Jim has ambivalent feelings about Basie, perceiving him as "a parasite" feeding "on the succulent terrain of the prison camps." Yet he is sometimes generous to Jim. For instance, he is the only one who gives him presents on his birthday. In addition, his confidence in the future is encouraging. However, when Jim runs into Basie and a group of bandits outside the stadium, he recognizes that "Basie had been prepared to see him die, and only Jim's lavish descriptions of the booty waiting for the bandits in the stadium ... sustained Basie's interest in Jim."

At the end of their relationship, Basie remains "the same small, finicky man ... ignoring everything but the shortest-term advantage. His one strength was that he never allowed himself to dream, because he had never been able to take anything for granted." That is why he survives so long, because the entire experience of the war had "barely touched" him.

Father

Jim's father, a serious man, tries to remain calm in the face of threats to his firm from the Communist Labor Unions, his concern for his work with the British Residents Association, and fears for Jim and his mother.

Frank

An American sailor Jim meets as he wanders around Shanghai looking for his parents, Frank introduces Jim to Basie.

Vera Frankel

Vera is Jim's nanny at Amherst Avenue, who usually follows Jim everywhere "like a guard dog." She is "a calm girl who never smiled and found everything strange about Jim and his parents." Her family fled Poland after Hitler's invasion. They now live with thousands of Jewish refugees in "a gloomy district of tenements and faded apartment blocks." The fact that she and her parents all live together in one room amazes and fascinates Jim.

Jim

The novel, opening from the eve of the Japanese attack on Pearl Harbor on December 7,

1941, focuses on the story of Jim, an eleven-year-old British boy who lives with his family in Shanghai. Before the Japanese take over Shanghai, Jim lives a comfortable life in the city's suburbs. He has seen some of the devastating results of the war, but seems to be detached from them. Completely absorbed in his own privileged world, he spends his days riding his bicycle around the city, dreaming of being a fighter pilot like the Japanese pilots he sees flying overhead. When he is separated from his parents after the Japanese take over the city, his world drastically changes.

At the detention center, Jim's bravery emerges as he learns important survival skills. On his way to the prison camp, Jim "already felt himself apart from the others, who had behaved as passively as the Chinese peasants. Jim realized that he was closer to the Japanese, who had seized Shanghai and sunk the American fleet at Pearl Harbor," pilots "ready to chance everything on little more than their own will." At this point, Jim retains his romantic dreams of heroism.

During his three years at the prison camp, Jim exhibits his strength, his curiosity, his energy, and his eagerness to please. Early on, he decides he won't allow himself to become too ill and so is able to perform countless errands for others. He enjoys the idea that his errands help keep the others alive. He works hard in order "to keep the camp going." Dr. Ransome often refers to him as a "free spirit" roving across the camp, "hunting down some new idea in his head."

He is curious about everything, including the war. He discovers what it takes to survive, learning how to get extra food and how to fight those who would try to take his rations. While trying to keep himself alive, he sometimes takes food meant for others and feels guilty, acknowledging that "parts of his mind and body frequently separated themselves from each other."

Jim's experiences in the camp change him from an innocent boy to an experienced man. He learns to accept the cruelty he sees around him and comes to understand the true horror of war. Yet he also learns that "having someone to care for was the same as being cared for by someone else."

Private Kimura

A Japanese guard at the camp who sometimes invites Jim into his bungalow and allows him to wear his armor.

Dr. Lockwood

Dr. Lockwood is the Vice-Chairman of the British Residents Association. He throws elaborate parties, including the "fancy-dress Christmas" party Jim and his family go to at the beginning of the novel.

Mr. Maxted

Mr. Maxted is the father of Jim's closest friend,

Patrick. Jim admired this architect-turned-entrepreneur who had designed the Metropole Theater and numerous Shanghai nightclubs. He imagined himself growing up like Mr. Maxted, "the perfect type of the Englishman who had adapted himself to Shanghai, something that Jim's father, with his seriousness of mind, had never really done."

Mr. Maxted is also sent to Lunghua Camp where he helps distribute food to the prisoners. Jim runs errands for him in the camp and cares for him during the trek to the Olympic Stadium "out of nostalgia for his childhood dream of growing up one day to be like him." Mr. Maxted is also kind to Jim at the camp and encourages him to continue on the march when Jim is about to give in to death. Mr. Maxted dies soon after they get there.

Mother

Jim's mother is "a gentle and clever woman whose main purposes in life, he had decided, were to go to parties and help him with his Latin homework." After the war, when she and Jim's father return to Amherst Avenue, they take a long time to recover from their experience at the prison camp. When Jim is reunited with his parents, he decides they are too worn out from their own experiences in the camp to hear about his experiences.

Lieutenant Price

Price takes over Lunghua Camp after the Japanese leave. He shoots Private Kimura.

Dr. Ransome

When Jim first meets Dr. Ransome, the British doctor in the camp, Ransome is in his late twenties, with "the self-assured manner of the Royal Navy officers" Jim had seen at the parties. At first, Jim distrusts him and perceives Ransome as selfish and arrogant. On the way to the camp, Jim notices that the doctor is "less interested in the dying old people than he pretended."

Media Adaptations

- *Empire of the Sun* was adapted as a film in 1987. Tom Stoppard and Menno Meyjes (uncredited) wrote the screenplay and Steven Spielberg produced and directed it for Warner

Bros.

In the camp, however, Jim's opinion of him changes. He still considers him selfish, but on occasion the doctor begins to reveal his generosity and spirit of self-sacrifice when he often gives Jim some of his own food. He also takes an interest in Jim's education, always coming up with homework problems for him to complete. Due to this kindness, Jim is determined to keep Dr. Ransome alive. While he shows obvious affection for Jim, he "resented [him] for revealing an obvious truth about the war, that people were only too able to adapt to it."

Mr. Tullock

Mr. Tullock is the chief mechanic at the Packard agency in Shanghai. He lets Jim come back into the camp and keeps him out of Price's way.

Mrs. Vincent

Jim shares a room at the camp with Mrs. Vincent, her husband, and their six-year-old son. She resents his presence and makes him feel unwelcome. In fact, she seems detached from everything around her, even her own son. Jim often has adolescent sexual fantasies about her. By the end of their stay at the camp, Jim grants her a certain respect, deciding she is "one of the few people in Lunghua Camp who appreciated the humor of it all." Mrs. Vincent dies in the march back from the stadium.

Yang

Yang is Jim's "fast-talking" chauffeur.

Themes

Coming of Age

The main focus of *Empire of the Sun* is Jim's maturation from child to man during World War II. After the war begins and he is separated from his parents, he spends the remainder of the book trying to reunite with them. He learns to survive the brutal conditions he faces in detention and prison camps. As a result of these experiences, he learns important lessons about himself and human nature.

Change and Transformation

As Ballard traces Jim's maturation, he explores the transformations he experiences. The biggest change occurs when Jim is wrenched from his comfortable, privileged life in Shanghai and forced to live, as do the Chinese, with deprivation and the constant threat of death. This experience brings Jim to new levels of self-discovery as he realizes his ingenuity, courage, and resilience in the face of tragedy.

Alienation and Loneliness

Jim must learn to cope with the alienation and loneliness that result when he is separated from his parents. As an only child, Jim had used his imagination to fill lonely days, envisioning himself as a Japanese fighter pilot. His imagination also helped Jim combat the loneliness he suffered after losing his parents.

While in camp, Jim tries to erase his sense of alienation through his interaction with the other prisoners. He considers the prisoners to be almost an extended family, and thus comes to feel a measure of safety while he is interned there. In this way, he tries to create order in a chaotic and dangerous world.

Topics for Further Study

- Research the internment of European civilians in China by the Japanese during World War II. Can you find reports of experiences similar to or different from those of Jim's?

- Investigate what psychologists say about the relationship between prisoners and guards. Compare their findings to the dynamics of Jim's relationship with his guards. Find examples in the novel.
- View the film *Empire of the Sun*. What differences do you find between the book and the movie? What effect do those differences have on the themes? Characters?
- Investigate the culture of Japan and China. Compare your findings to Jim's descriptions of the different cultures.

Strength and Weakness

Jim's ability to cope with his harsh surroundings reveals his strength of character and the nature of human adaptability. While others escape through death, Jim resolves to survive. In order to do this, he learns how to eat insects and to ingratiate himself with his captors.

Violence and Cruelty

Jim is able to recognize the capacity for violence and cruelty in others as well as himself. After seeing so much cruelty, Jim comes to understand its causes. For example, "Jim knew that

Lieutenant Price would have liked to get him alone and then beat him to death, not because he was cruel, but because only the sight of Jim's agony would clear away all the pain that he himself had endured."

Jim often struggles with his own capacity for cruelty. In order to survive, he obtains extra food, which sometimes means less for others. He also learns how to defend himself against others trying to take food from him. As a result, "few boys of his own age dared to touch" him and "few men." Sometimes stealing food makes him feel guilty and he acknowledges that "parts of his mind and body frequently separated themselves from each other."

Appearances and Reality

By the end of the novel, Jim has let go of his innocent ideas about the nature of war. As a child, he had considered war to be "an heroic adventure filled with scenes of sacrifice and stoicism, of countless acts of bravery" like those detailed on the newsreels he watches and the magazines he reads. By the end of the novel, however, Jim recognizes the devastating reality of war.

Style

Point of View

One of the novel's most interesting and successful qualities is its use of point of view. The events unfold through the eyes of Jim, the protagonist, as he experiences the horrors of life in China during World War II. While providing a vivid depiction of the destruction that surrounds him, Jim remains the detached observer, a survival skill he learns at the prison camp. That same sense of detachment is evident in the novel's early scenes before Jim is separated from his parents.

While he enjoys the benefits of his upper class life in Shanghai, this lonely boy observes with an ironic eye the stark contrasts between European and Chinese life. He notes the "dances and garden parties, the countless bottles of scotch consumed in aid of the war effort" while beggars are whipped in the streets by limousine drivers. Jim sees that "all over the western suburbs people were wearing fancy dress, as if Shanghai had become a city of clowns."

Genre

Although this novel is concerned with the devastating impact of war, it does contain elements found in the science fiction genre. In their review published in *Newsweek*, David Lehman and Donna

Foote maintain that the novel has "more in common with [Ballard's science fiction novels] than immediately meets the eye. Like its predecessors, the book explores the zone of 'inner space' that Ballard sees as 'the true domain of science fiction.'" John Gross echoes this assessment in his review for *The New York Times*, viewing many of its scenes "lurid and bizarre, so very nearly out of this world."

Symbol

In the novel, Ballard uses abandoned buildings and drained swimming pools as symbols of Jim's predicament and psychological state. As he searches for his parents in Shanghai, Jim comes across the abandoned homes and drained swimming pools, symbols of the privileged lives of the Europeans who once resided there. These empty images foreshadow the world Jim will face in the prison camp, a world where social hierarchies reverse and eventually collapse.

Historical Context

World War II

The rise of totalitarian regimes in Germany, Italy, and Japan during the 1930s tipped the scales toward a world war. These dictatorships—known as the Axis power when they became allies—began to forcibly expand into neighboring countries. For instance, in 1936 Benito Mussolini's Italian troops took over Ethiopia, which gave them a strong foothold in Africa. In 1938 Germany annexed Austria; a year later, German forces occupied Czechoslovakia. Italy took control of Albania in 1939.

On September 1, 1939, Germany invaded Poland and World War II began. On September 3, 1939, Britain and France declared war on Germany after a U-boat sank the British ship *Athenia* off the coast of Ireland. Another British ship, *Courageous*, was sunk on September 19. All the members of the British Commonwealth, except Ireland, soon joined Britain and France in their declaration of war.

By 1940, Japan controlled a large part of China, including Northern China, the coastal areas, and the Yangtze valley. During the years before World War II, the Japanese met resistance from the Chinese Communists. After Japan attacked U.S. and British bases in 1941 and World War II broke out in Asia, China received U.S. and British aid.

By the end of the war, however, China was in full civil war. Hostilities between the Chinese nationalist forces and the communist troops intensified into a full-scale war as both sides vied for occupancy of the territories evacuated by the Japanese. By April 1950, China was a communist country.

In August 1937 the Japanese attacked Shanghai, which fell under Japanese control by November. The foreign zones of the city were occupied by the Japanese after December 7, 1941, the date *Empire of the Sun* opens. In 1943 Great Britain and the United States gave up their claims in Shanghai. China regained control of the city at the end of World War II. In May 1949, Shanghai fell to the Communists.

Critical Overview

Published in 1984, *Empire of the Sun* was highly acclaimed by critics and became a bestseller in England. In their review of the novel appearing in *Newsweek*, David Lehman and Donna Foote place the book "on anyone's short list of outstanding novels inspired by the second world war.... [It] combines the exactness of an autobiographical testament with the hallucinatory atmosphere of twilight-zone fiction."

Most reviews focus on the novel's serious subject matter. John Calvin Batchelor, in his essay, "A Boy Saved by the Bomb" in *The New York Times Book Review*, asserts that Ballard "has reached into the events of his childhood to create a searing and frightening tale of wartime China. Yet this novel is much more than the gritty story of a child's miraculous survival in the grimly familiar setting of World War II's concentration camps. There is no nostalgia for a good war here, no sentimentality for the human spirit at extremes.... He aims to render a vision of the apocalypse, and succeeds so well that it can hurt to dwell upon his images."

In his review of the novel for *The New York Times*, John Gross contends that the book "sets out to raise large issues and stir deep feelings, and for the most part it succeeds remarkably well." After criticizing what he considers to be Ballard's editorializing at the end of the book, Gross claims "that is the only real weakness in an outstanding novel."

Gross also praises the novel's style: "The detail of life both in the city and in the camp is brilliantly rendered by Mr. Ballard—with swift, economic strokes where there could easily have been clutter, with a plain, terse style where rhetoric would have been counterproductive."

In *Books and Bookmen*, William Boyd claims that "what makes [this] Ballard's best novel is that on this occasion style and narrative fuse." Boyd praises the author's pace, structure, character development and use of symbols. While he asserts that the novel contains "flaws" like "shaky" dialogue and repetition in some parts, he states that "the mix is otherwise extremely—and uniquely in his work—impressive."

Many critics maintain that the novel has strong ties to the science-fiction genre. Lehman and Foote note that the novel has earned Ballard the kind of critical acclaim denied his earlier work, "since it has more in common with them than immediately meets the eye. Like its predecessors, the book explores the zone of 'inner space' that Ballard sees as 'the true domain of science fiction.'"

Although the novel is clearly more realistic than Ballard's past work, Gross "still hesitates to call [it] a conventional novel ... because many of the scenes in it are so lurid and bizarre, so very nearly out of this world. Among other things, they help to explain why in his work up till now Mr. Ballard should have been repeatedly drawn to apocalyptic themes."

Considering Ballard's future, David Pringle in *Earth Is the Alien Planet: J. G. Ballard's Four Dimensional Nightmare* determines that "Ballard's reputation will grow in the decades to come, and he is likely to become recognized as by far and away the most important literary figure associated with the field of science fiction. More than that, he will be seen as one of the major imaginative writers of the second half of the 20th century—an author for our times, and for the future."

Sources

John Calvin Batchelor, "A Boy Saved by the Bomb," in *The New York Times Book Review*, November 11, 1984, p. 11.

William Boyd, "Unique Vision," in *Books and Bookmen*, September, 1984, pp. 12-13.

John Gross, "A Survivor's Narrative," in *The New York Times* October 13, 1984, p. 18.

David Lehman and Donna Foote, in a review in *Newsweek*, January 28, 1985, p. 69.

David Pringle, in *Earth Is the Alien Planet: J. G. Ballard's Four Dimensional Nightmare*, Borgo Press, 1979.

For Further Study

Jonathan Cott, "The Strange Visions of J. G. Ballard," in *Rolling Stone*, November 19, 1987, p. 76.

> In this interview, Ballard discusses how the novel relates to the science fiction genre.

Edward Fox, "Goodbye, Cruel World," in *The Nation*, Vol. 240, No. 3, January 26, 1985, pp. 89-90.

> This review explores the theme of survival in the novel.

Roger Luckhurst, "Petition, Repetition, and 'Autobiography': J. G. Ballard's *Empire of the Sun* and *The Kindness of Women*," *Contemporary Literature*, Vol. 35, Winter, 1994, pp. 688-708.

> Luckhurst examines the autobiographical significance in both novels.

Luc Sante, "Tales from the Dark Side," *The New York Times Magazine*, September 9, 1990, p. 58.

> Sante explores the "complex, obsessive, and disquieting" themes in the novel.

John Simon, in a review in *National Review*, February 5, 1988, p. 59.

Simon finds the cinematic adaptation a poor version of the novel.

Lightning Source UK Ltd.
Milton Keynes UK
UKHW020001201120
373714UK00016B/327